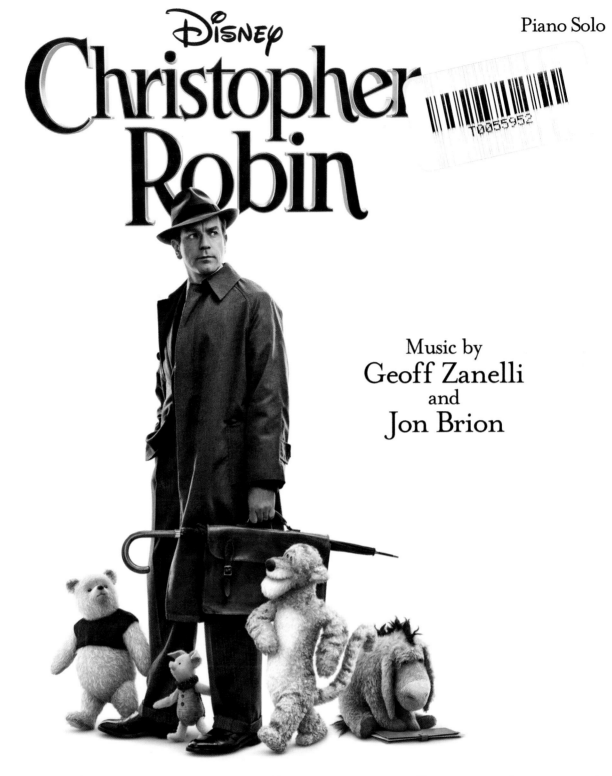

Disney
Christopher Robin

Music by
Geoff Zanelli
and
Jon Brion

Music from the Motion Picture Soundtrack

Disney Characters and Artwork TM & © 2018 Disney

Based on the "Winnie the Pooh" works by A.A. Milne and E.H. Shepard.

ISBN 978-1-5400-3782-4

HAL•LEONARD®

Visit Hal Leonard Online at
www.halleonard.com

Contact Us:
Hal Leonard
7777 West Bluemound Road
Milwaukee, WI 53213
Email: info@halleonard.com

In Europe contact:
Hal Leonard Europe Limited
Distribution Centre, Newmarket Road
Bury St Edmunds, Suffolk, IP33 3YB
Email: info@halleonardeurope.com

In Australia contact:
Hal Leonard Australia Pty. Ltd.
4 Lentara Court
Cheltenham, Victoria, 3192 Australia
Email: info@halleonard.com.au

Contents

8   Storybook

10   Goodbye, Farewell

16   Not Doing Nothing Anymore

18   Evelyn Goes It Alone

13   Through the Tree

22   Heffalump Battle

25   My Favorite Day

28   Busy Doing Nothing

30   Christopher Robin

STORYBOOK

Music by GEOFF ZANELLI

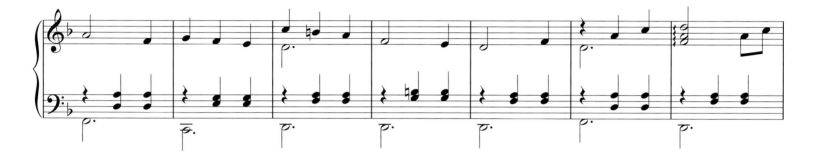

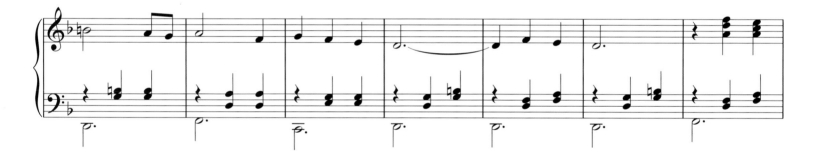

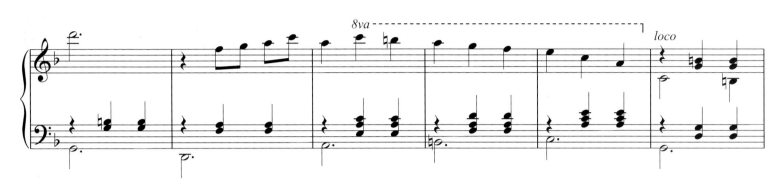

GOODBYE, FAREWELL

Music and Lyrics by
RICHARD M. SHERMAN

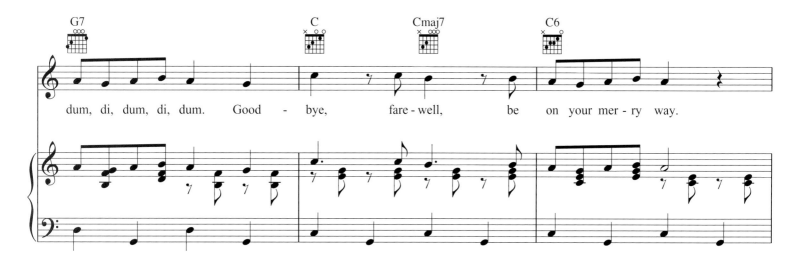

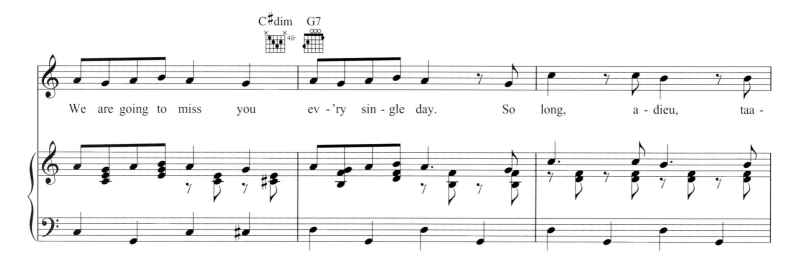

taa and too - dle - oo. On my mer - ry way I'll al - ways think of you. On

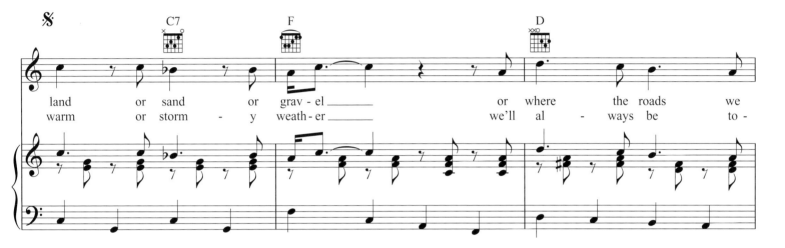

land or sand or grav - el _____ or where the roads we
warm or storm - y weath - er _____ we'll al - ways be to -

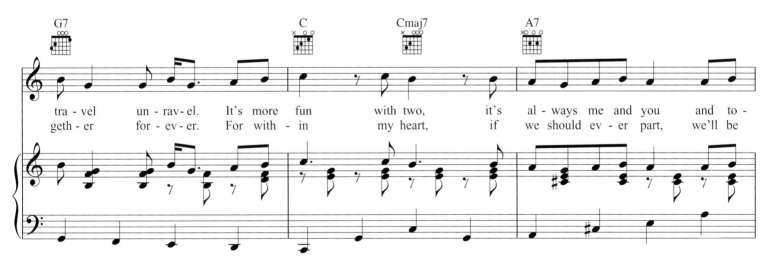

tra - vel un - rav - el. It's more fun with two, it's al - ways me and you and to -
geth - er for - ev - er. For with - in my heart, if we should ev - er part, we'll be

To Coda ⊕

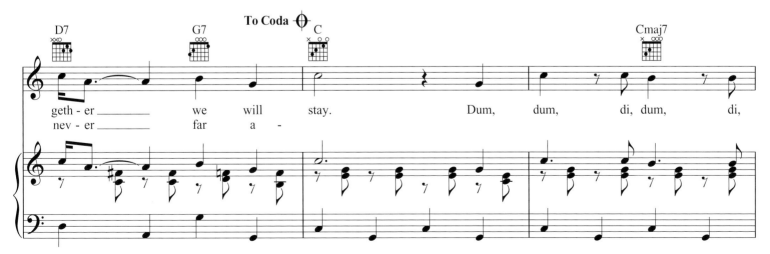

geth - er _____ we will stay. Dum, dum, di, dum, di,
nev - er _____ far a -

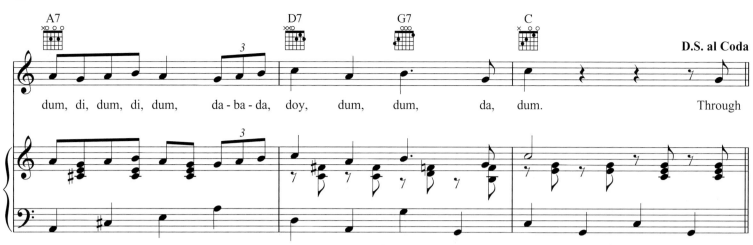

D.S. al Coda

dum, di, dum, di, dum, da - ba - da, doy, dum, dum, da, dum. Through

CODA

way from each oth - er. We'll be nev - er_____ far a - way. Dum,

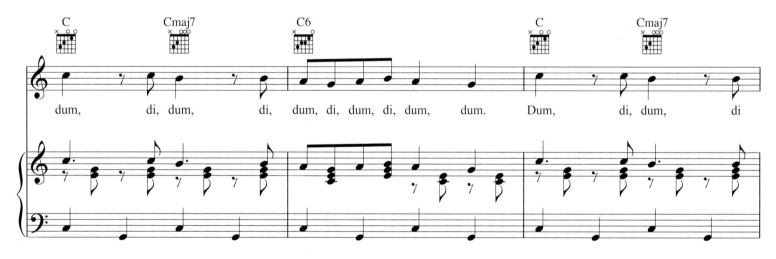

dum, di, dum, di, dum, di, dum, di, dum, dum. Dum, di, dum, di

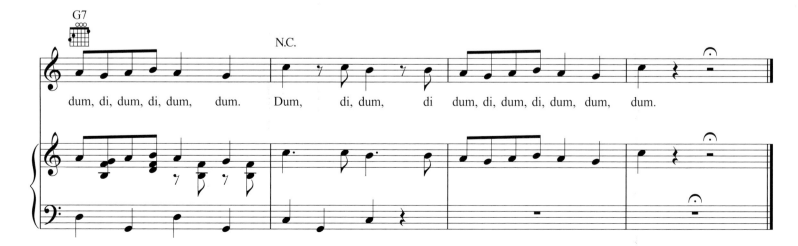

dum, di, dum, di, dum, dum. Dum, di, dum, di dum, di, dum, di, dum, dum, dum.

THROUGH THE TREE

Music by GEOFF ZANELLI

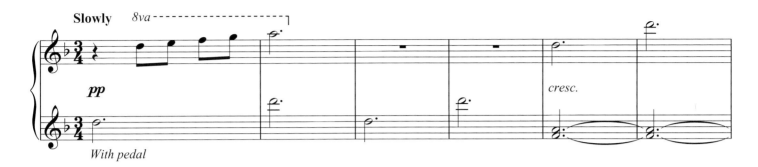

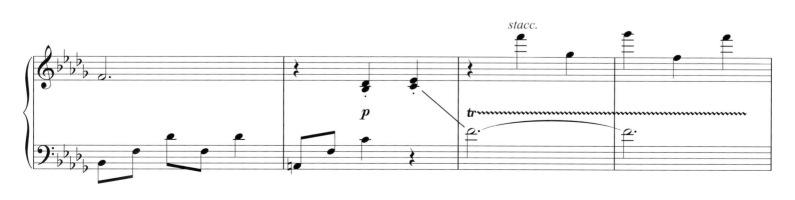

NOT DOING NOTHING ANYMORE

Music by JON BRION

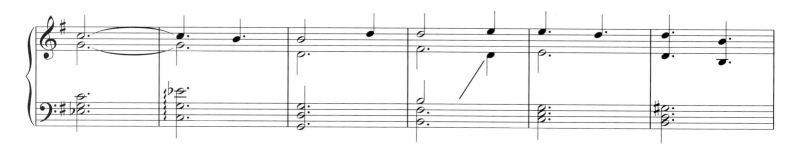

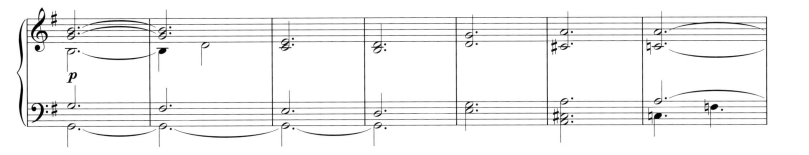

EVELYN GOES IT ALONE

Music by GEOFF ZANELLI

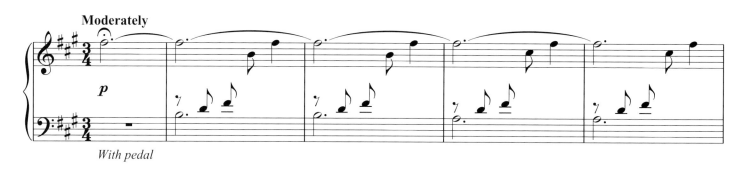

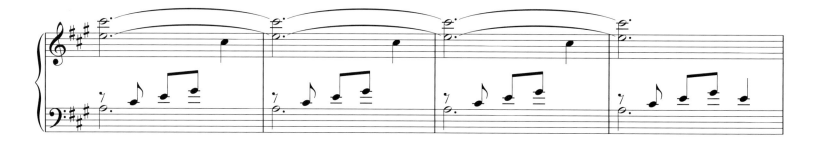

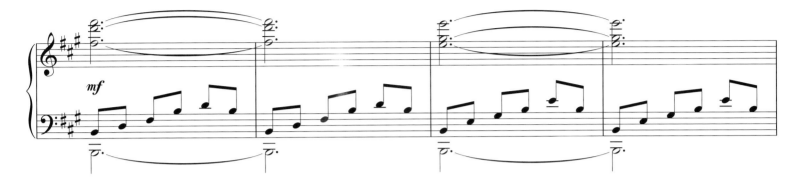

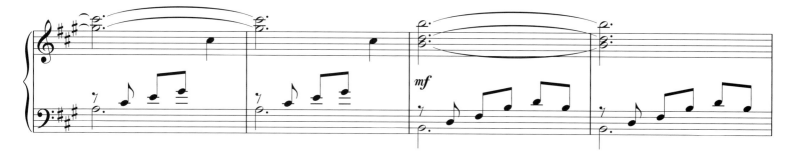

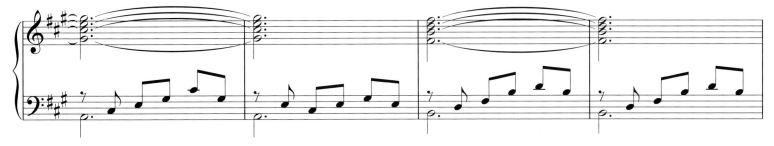

HEFFALUMP BATTLE

Music by JON BRION

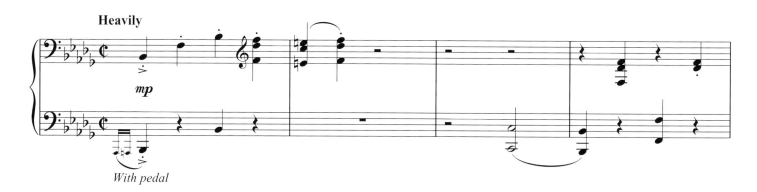

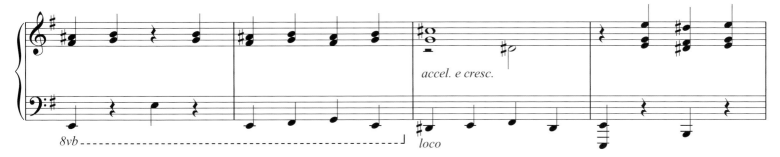

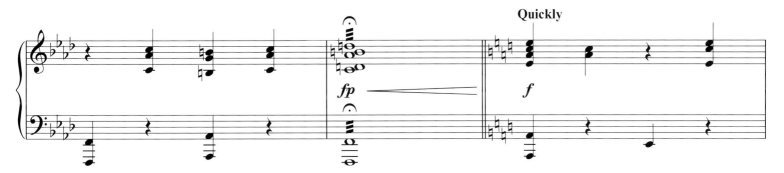

Quickly

molto rall.

MY FAVORITE DAY

Music by GEOFF ZANELLI
and JON BRION

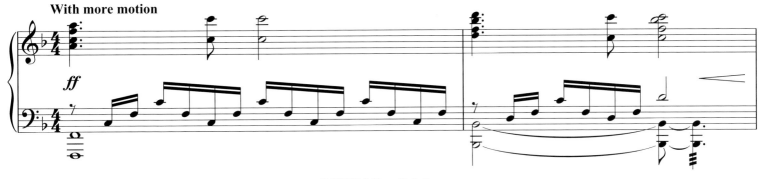

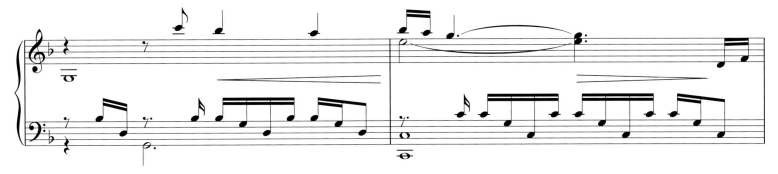

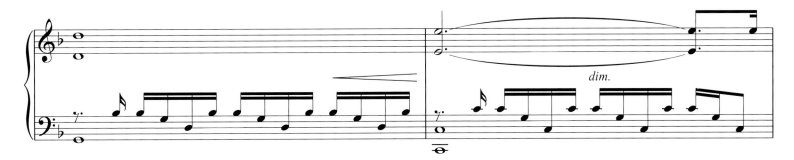

BUSY DOING NOTHING

Music and Lyrics by
RICHARD M. SHERMAN

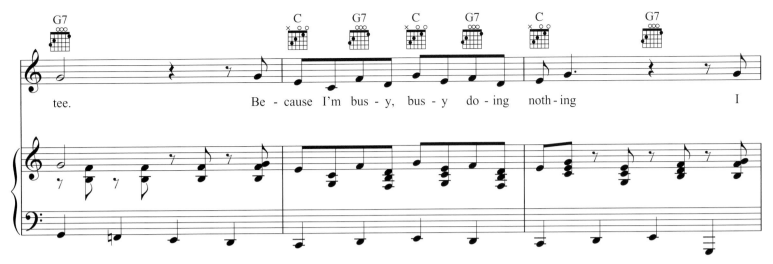

tee. Be - cause I'm bus - y, bus - y do - ing noth - ing I

find I nev - er find _____ the time _ to rest. Be - ing

bus - y do - ing noth - ing, I'm bus - y do - ing some - thing. Do - ing

noth - ing is the some - thing I do best.

CHRISTOPHER ROBIN

Music and Lyrics by
RICHARD M. SHERMAN

Moderately, with freedom

Chris - to - pher Rob - in, look at me;

tell me what you see. ____ Do you re - mem - ber how we used to

be? You were a spe - cial friend of mine.

* Recorded a half step lower.

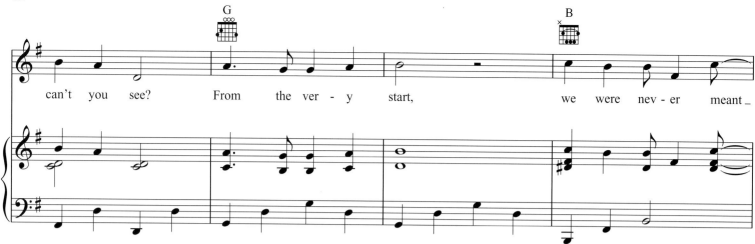

can't you see? From the ver - y start, we were nev - er meant _

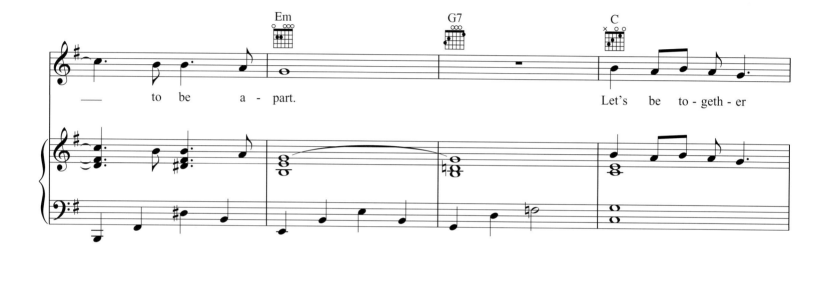

_ to be a - part. Let's be to - geth - er

ev - 'ry day, play - ing the games _ we al - ways play.

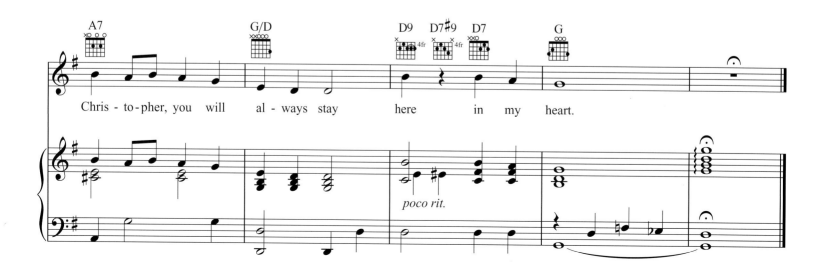

Chris - to - pher, you will al - ways stay here in my heart.

poco rit.